CAUSES AND EFFECTS
OF THE
TEXAS REVOLUTION

Therese Harasymiw

New York

Published in 2010 by The Rosen Publishing Group, Inc.
29 East 21st Street, New York, NY 10010

Book Design: Michael J. Flynn

Photo Credits: Cover (battle scene), pp. 11 (1833 map), 25 (both) © Texas State Library and Archives Commission; cover, pp. 3, 4, 6, 8, 12, 14, 18, 22, 24, 28, 30, 31, 32 (Texas emblem on all), 3–32 (textured background), 5 (mission), 7 (feather design), 15 (white flag), back cover (Texas flag) Shutterstock.com; pp. 4 (Cabeza de Vaca), 24 (Sam Houston) © MPI/Hulton Archive/Getty Images; pp. 6 (Hidalgo), 27 (annexation cartoon) Library of Congress Prints and Photographs Division; pp. 8 (Stephen Austin), 19 (David Crockett), 20 (Sam Houston) © Hulton Archive/Getty Images; p. 9 (Austin and colonist) © Bettmann/Corbis; pp. 11 (map inset), 23 (map) © GeoAtlas; p. 13 (Antonio López de Santa Anna) © The San Jacinto Museum of History, Houston; p. 14 (cannon), 17 (Martín Perfecto de Cos), 17 (mission), 26 (Mirabeau B. Lamar) Wikimedia Commons; p. 18 (battle at the Alamo) © Kean Collection/Hulton Archive/Getty Images; p. 19 (battle at the Alamo) © Friends of the Governor's Mansion; p. 21 (Declaration) © Broadsides Collection, Earl Vandale Collection, Center for American History, University of Texas at Austin.

Library of Congress Cataloging-in-Publication Data

Harasymiw, Therese.
Causes and effects of the Texas revolution / Therese Harasymiw.
     p. cm. — (Spotlight on Texas)
Includes index.
 ISBN 978-1-61532-466-8 (pbk.)
 ISBN: 978-1-61532-467-5 (6-pack)
 ISBN 978-1-61532-468-2 (library binding)
1. Texas—History—Revolution, 1835-1836—Juvenile literature. 2. Texas—History—To 1846—Juvenile literature. I. Title.
 F390.H275 2010
 976.4'01—dc22
                              2009031346

Manufactured in the United States of America

CPSIA Compliance Information: Batch # WW1ORC: For further information contact Rosen Publishing, New York, New York at 1-800-237-9932.

CONTENTS

THE FIRST TEXANS

Texas wasn't always part of the United States. Earlier, it was its own country. Before that, it was a Mexican state. Even earlier, Spain claimed Texas and Mexico. Texas has changed hands many times.

Let's start at the beginning. Native Americans were the first Texans. They lived there for thousands of years before European **explorers** arrived.

Lost in a New Land

Álvar Núñez Cabeza de Vaca was part of a lost group of Spanish explorers. In 1528, they landed near Galveston, Texas. Cabeza de Vaca lived with Native Americans for several years. First he was a slave. Then he became a trader and healer. Cabeza de Vaca grew to respect the Native American way of life. He later wrote a book about his adventures.

In 1528, Spanish explorers traveled through Texas and Mexico. They hoped to find gold and other riches in the area they claimed. They called this area "New Spain."

In the late 1600s, French explorers claimed southeastern Texas. The Spanish wanted to strengthen their claim to the land and spread their **religion**. They began building **missions**. In 1803, the United States bought a large piece of land called the Louisiana Territory from France. This land included parts of eastern and northern Texas.

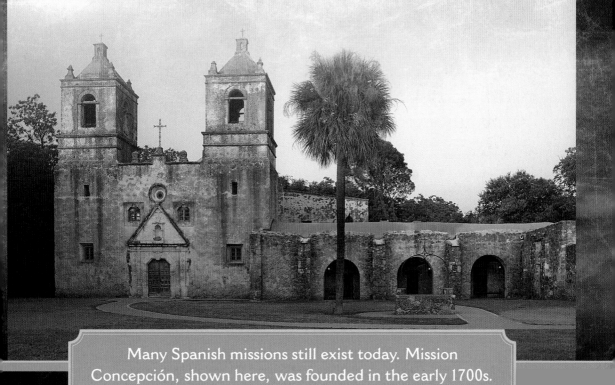

Many Spanish missions still exist today. Mission Concepción, shown here, was founded in the early 1700s.

MEXICAN WAR FOR INDEPENDENCE

On September 16, 1810, a group of Mexicans called for independence from Spain. Their leader, Father Miguel Hidalgo, was killed the next year. The Mexicans battled the Spanish colonial government for many years. Finally, in 1821, Spain agreed to free Mexico, which included Texas.

Although Mexico was independent, it was not at peace. Native Americans had struggled to keep their lands since the arrival of European explorers. They continued fighting after Mexico gained independence. The country was also very poor. It needed more trade and business opportunities.

Miguel Hidalgo

On September 16, 1810, Father Hidalgo rang his church bell to call people to fight. September 16 is honored today as Mexican Independence Day.

Native Americans in the United States

As in Mexico, Native Americans in the United States were losing their land. In some places, they were forced onto reservations. These were pieces of land set aside for Native Americans. Many fought to keep their land, but they had no chance against the U.S. military. In the southeast, some Native Americans began to live among the settlers and adopt their ways.

The government invited outsiders to settle in Mexican Texas. Men called empresarios (ehm-preh-SAHR-yohz) were given land if they promised to bring settlers with them. The government hoped the settlers would farm and increase trade. The settlers were meant to drive out the Native Americans, too.

Americans Come to Texas

Moses Austin of Missouri was the first empresario. He died before he could lead settlers to Mexican Texas. Stephen F. Austin carried out his father's plans. He led several hundred families to an area near the Brazos and Colorado rivers in 1822.

Native Americans' anger grew as they were pushed off their lands. The Mexican government told settlers to form **militias** to guard themselves against the Native Americans.

Only one empresario was born in Mexico. All others were American. American settlers soon outnumbered Mexican-born settlers. By 1830, Mexican president Anastacio Bustamante worried that the United States would annex, or take over, Texas. He passed laws to stop this from happening. The new laws angered the people of Texas.

Stephen Austin

An Early Call to War

In 1826, brothers Haden and Benjamin Edwards called for a war against Mexico. However, Mexican soldiers stopped the fighting with the help of Stephen Austin's militia. Most Texans didn't want war with Mexico at that time.

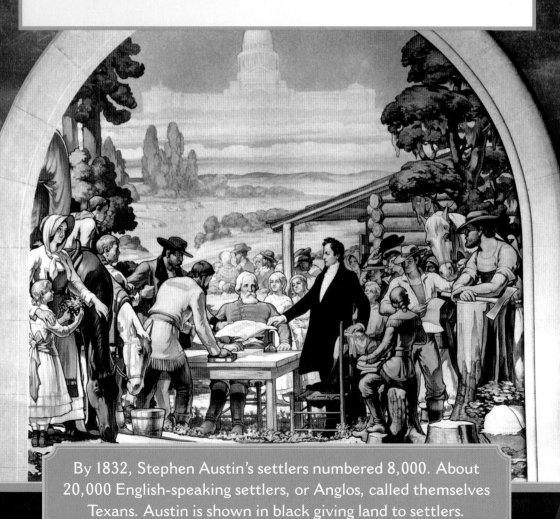

By 1832, Stephen Austin's settlers numbered 8,000. About 20,000 English-speaking settlers, or Anglos, called themselves Texans. Austin is shown in black giving land to settlers.

President Bustamante's Law of April 6, 1830 brought great change to Mexican Texas. Some parts of the law especially troubled Texans. One stopped more American empresarios from bringing settlers into Texas. Another taxed goods entering Texas from the United States. Yet another part of the law ended the movement of slaves into Texas.

In 1833, some Anglo settlers held a **convention**. They prepared a list of things they wanted from the Mexican government. They wanted the law withdrawn. They also wanted to form their own state. After Mexican independence from Spain, Texas had been joined with the state of Coahuila (koh-ah-WEE-lah). The capital of the new state was far away. It was hard for Texans to take part in this government.

This map from 1833 shows the Mexican state of Coahuila and Texas. You can also see the Austin settlement shown in dark pink.

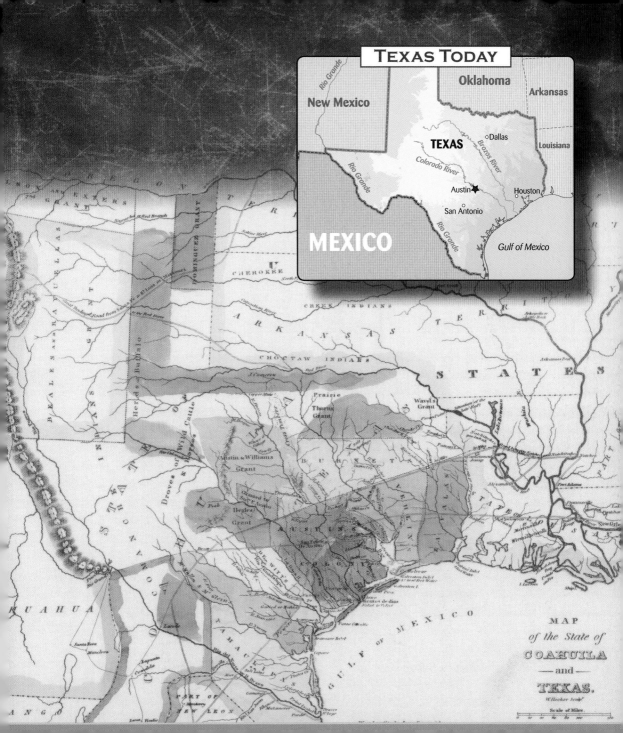

TEXAS TODAY

New Mexico

Oklahoma

Arkansas

Rio Grande

TEXAS

Dallas

Brazos River

Louisiana

Colorado River

Austin

Houston

San Antonio

Rio Grande

MEXICO

Gulf of Mexico

MAP
of the State of
COAHUILA
— and —
TEXAS.
W. Hooker Sculp.
Scale of Miles

SANTA ANNA TAKES CONTROL

In 1833, Mexican general Antonio López de Santa Anna took the Mexican presidency by force. Texas militias helped Santa Anna's soldiers. Texans hoped the new president would help them.

Stephen Austin traveled to Mexico City. He presented the Texans' wish for a separate state. Santa Anna feared the United States would annex a separate Texas easily. He said no. He also worried that Austin would lead a **rebellion**. Santa Anna jailed him for 2 years.

In 1834, Santa Anna began to seize power from all Mexican state governments. He made himself into a **dictator**. His actions angered people across Mexico. Anglos and Mexican-born Texans prepared to stand against him.

Antonio López de Santa Anna was a general. He first became famous fighting against Spain. His popularity helped him become president of Mexico.

Antonio López de Santa Anna

THE REVOLUTION BEGINS

Santa Anna sent troops into Texas in October 1835. His forces arrived first at the town of Gonzales. Their task was to take back a Mexican cannon given to the town to guard against Native American attacks. There were only eighteen men to defend the town. However, the people of Gonzales refused to give up the cannon. Stories say one of them cried, "Come and take it!"

A call for help brought more Texans to fight for Gonzales. The first shots of the Texas **Revolution** were fired there. After a short battle, the Mexican forces went to San Antonio without the cannon.

Across Texas, people realized the time had come for action. They used supplies from the state's militias to form an army.

COME AND TAKE IT

This cannon began the Texas Revolution. The words "come and take it" were sewn onto a flag and flown in battle.

At first, three men led the Texas army: Stephen Austin, James Bowie, and James Fannin Jr. They won several battles at the beginning. The Texans captured Goliad on October 10, 1835. Shortly after, the Texas army began a **siege** of San Antonio. Two battles during this time were the Battle of Concepción and the Grass Fight. The Texans won both. They controlled San Antonio by December 8.

Santa Anna's anger grew. He decided to lead his own forces. He had about 8,000 soldiers under his command. His first aim was to take back San Antonio.

Santa Anna arrived at San Antonio in February 1836. The Texans were surprised. They thought he would not attack until spring. A small force gathered within the San Antonio de Valero Mission. This mission was also known as the Alamo.

General Martín Perfecto de Cos led the Mexican soldiers at Goliad. He was married to Santa Anna's sister.

Martín Perfecto de Cos

Mission La Bahía del Espíritu Santo
Goliad, Texas

TAKE NO PRISONERS

Some Texans wanted to withdraw from San Antonio because they were outnumbered. However, James Bowie and William Barret Travis wanted to guard the mission until more help came. On February 23, 1836, Santa Anna began a siege of the Alamo. Travis wrote a letter for help. The letter was printed in a newspaper. Still, only about 200 soldiers stood against Santa Anna. The Mexican soldiers numbered between 1,000 and 6,000.

The Alamo became a symbol of the fight for Texas freedom. "Remember the Alamo!" became a battle cry of the Texas Revolution.

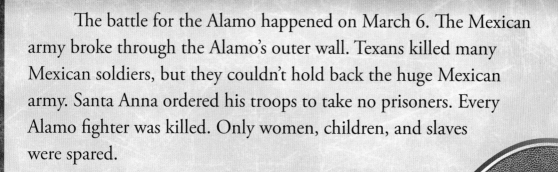

The battle for the Alamo happened on March 6. The Mexican army broke through the Alamo's outer wall. Texans killed many Mexican soldiers, but they couldn't hold back the huge Mexican army. Santa Anna ordered his troops to take no prisoners. Every Alamo fighter was killed. Only women, children, and slaves were spared.

Crockett's Last Adventure

David Crockett was born in Tennessee in 1786. He was a well-known pioneer, hunter, and soldier. Crockett was famous for telling stories about his adventures in the wild. He was elected to Congress in 1827, 1829, and 1833. He answered the call to battle at the Alamo and died fighting there. Crockett's life became the subject of many books and movies.

David Crockett

While the Battle of the Alamo was being fought, Texas leaders gathered in the town of Washington-on-the-Brazos. They wrote a **declaration** of independence and signed it on March 2, 1836. The officials also wrote a **constitution**. It was much like the U.S. Constitution. Soon, news reached them of the loss at the Alamo.

Sam Houston

On March 20, a Mexican force stopped nearly 300 Texas soldiers near Goliad. Led by James Fannin Jr., the Texans **surrendered**. Santa Anna ordered them all killed. Texans now knew that surrender meant death. Sam Houston was now general of the Texas army. He moved his army east. He wanted to keep Santa Anna's forces from capturing the remaining army supplies.

The Texas Declaration of Independence listed reasons why the Texans chose freedom from Mexico. It said that the Mexican government was dishonest and wanted to harm Texas.

UNANIMOUS
DECLARATION OF INDEPENDENCE,

BY THE

DELEGATES OF THE PEOPLE OF TEXAS,

IN GENERAL CONVENTION,

AT THE TOWN OF WASHINGTON,

ON THE SECOND DAY OF MARCH, 1836.

When a government has ceased to protect the lives, liberty, and property of the people, from whom its legitimate powers are derived, and for the advancement of whose happiness it was instituted; and so far from being a guarantee for the enjoyment of those inestimable and inalienable rights, becomes an instrument in the hands of evil rulers for their oppression.

When the Federal Republican Constitution of their country, which they have sworn to support, no longer has a substantial existence, and the whole nature of their government has been forcibly changed, without their consent, from a restricted Federative Republic, composed of Sovereign States, to a consolidated Central Military despotism, in which every interest is disregarded but that of the army and the priesthood, both the eternal enemies of civil liberty, the ever ready minions of power, and the usual instruments of tyrants.

When, long after the spirit of the constitution has departed, moderation is at length so far lost by those in power, that even the semblance of freedom is removed, and the forms themselves of the constitution discontinued, and so far from their petitions and remonstrances being regarded, the agents who bear them and who dare to speak for the rights of the nation, are thrown into dungeons, and mercenary armies sent forth to force a new government upon them at the point of the bayonet.

When, in consequence of such acts of malfeasance and abduction on the part of the government, anarchy prevails, and civil society is dissolved into its original elements. In such a crisis, the first law of nature, the right of self preservation, the inherent and inalienable right of the people to appeal to first principles, and take their political affairs into their own hands in extreme cases, enjoins it as a right towards themselves, and a sacred obligation to their posterity, to abolish such government, and create another in its stead, calculated to rescue them from impending dangers, and to secure their welfare and happiness.

Nations, as well as individuals, are amenable for their acts to the public opinion of mankind. A statement of a part of our grievances is therefore submitted to an impartial world, in justification of the bazardous but unavoidable step now taken, of severing our political connection with the Mexican people, and assuming an independent attitude among the nations of the earth.

The Mexican Government, by its colonization laws, invited and induced the Anglo American population of Texas to colonize its wilderness under the pledged faith of a written constitution, that they should continue to enjoy that constitutional liberty and republican government to which they had been habituated in the land of their birth, the United States of America.

In this expectation they have been cruelly disappointed, inasmuch as the Mexican nation has acquiesced in the late changes made in the government by General Antonio Lopez Santa Anna, who having overturned the constitution of his country, now offers us the cruel alternative, either to abandon our homes acquired by so many privations, or submit to the most intolerable of all tyranny, the combined despotism of the sword and the priesthood.

It hath sacrificed our welfare to the state of Coahuila, by which our interests have been continually depressed through a jealous and partial course of legislation, carried on at a far distant seat of government, by a hostile majority, in an unknown tongue, and this too, notwithstanding we have petitioned in the humblest terms for the establishment of a separate state government, and have, in accordance with the provisions of the national constitution, presented to the general congress a republican constitution, which was, without just cause, contemptuously rejected.

It incarcerated in a dungeon, for a long time, one of our citizens, for no other cause but a zealous endeavour to procure the acceptance of our constitution and the establishment of a state government.

It has failed and refused to secure, on a firm basis, the right of trial by jury, that palladium of civil liberty and only safe guarantee for the life, liberty, and property of the citizen.

It has failed to establish any public system of education, although possessed of almost boundless resources, (the public domain;) and although it is an axiom in political science, that unless a people are educated and enlightened, it is idle to expect the continuance of civil liberty, or the capacity for self government.

It has suffered the military commandants, stationed among us, to exercise arbitrary acts of oppression and tyranny, thus trampling upon the most sacred rights of the citizen, and rendering the military superior to the civil power.

It has dissolved, by force of arms, the state congress of Coahuila and Texas, and obliged our representatives to fly for their lives from the seat of government, thus depriving us of the fundamental political right of representation.

It has demanded the surrender of a number of our citizens, and ordered military detachments to seize and carry them into the interior for trial, in contempt of the civil authorities, and in defiance of the laws and the constitution.

It has made piratical attacks upon our commerce, by commissioning foreign desperadoes, and authorizing them to seize our vessels, and convey the property of our citizens to far distant ports for confiscation.

It denies us the right of worshipping the Almighty according to the dictates of our own conscience, by the support of a National Religion, calculated to promote the temporal interest of its human functionaries, rather than the glory of the true and living God.

It has demanded us to deliver up our arms, which are essential to our defence—the rightful property of freemen—and formidable only to tyrannical governments.

It has invaded our country both by sea and by land, with the intent to lay waste our territory, and drive us from our homes; and has now a large mercenary army advancing, to carry on against us a war of extermination.

It has, through its emissaries, incited the merciless savage, with the tomahawk and scalping knife, to massacre the inhabitants of our defenceless frontiers.

It has been, during the whole time of our connection with it, the contemptible sport and victim of successive military revolutions, and hath continually exhibited every characteristic of a weak, corrupt, and tyrannical government.

These, and other grievances, were patiently borne by the people of Texas, until they reached that point at which forbearance ceases to be a virtue. We then took up arms in defence of the National Constitution. We appealed to our Mexican brethren for assistance; our appeal has been made in vain; though months have elapsed, no sympathetic response has yet been heard from the interior. We are therefore forced to the melancholy conclusion, that the Mexican people have acquiesced in the destruction of their liberty, and the substitution therefor of a military government; that they are unfit to be free, and incapable of self government.

The necessity of self-preservation, therefore, now decrees our eternal political separation.

We, therefore, the delegates, with plenary powers, of the people of Texas, in solemn convention assembled, appealing to a candid world for the necessities of our condition, do hereby resolve and DECLARE, that our political connection with the Mexican nation has forever ended, and that the people of Texas, do now constitute a FREE, SOVEREIGN, and INDEPENDENT REPUBLIC, and are fully invested with all the rights and attributes which properly belong to independent nations; and, conscious of the rectitude of our intentions, we fearlessly and confidently commit the issue to the decision of the supreme Arbiter of the destinies of nations.

RICHARD ELLIS, President.

C. B. STEWART, THOMAS BARNETT,	}	Austin.
JAS. COLLINSWORTH, EDWIN WALLER, ASA BRIGHAM, J. S. D. BYROM,	}	Brazoria.
FRANCISCO RUIS, ANTONIO NAVARO, JESSE B. BADGETT,	}	Bexar.
WILLIAM D. LACY, WILLIAM MENIFEE,	}	Colorado.
JAMES GAINES, W. CLARK, JR.,	}	Sabine.

JOHN FISHER, MATT. CALDWELL,	}	Gonzales.
WILLIAM MOTLEY, L. DE ZAVALA,	}	Goliad.
STEPH. H. EVERETT,	}	Harrisburgh.
GEORGE W. SMITH,	}	Jasper.
ELIJAH STAPP,	}	Jackson.
CLAIBORNE WEST, WILLIAM B. SCATES,	}	Jefferson.
M. B. MENARD, A. B. HARDIN,	}	Liberty.
BAILEY HARDIMAN,	}	Matagorda.

J. W. BUNTON, THOS. J. GAZELEY, R. M. COLEMAN,	}	Mina.
ROBERT POTTER, THOMAS J. RUSK, CH. S. TAYLOR, JOHN S. ROBERTS,	}	Nacogdoches.
ROBERT HAMILTON, COLLIN McKINNEY,	}	Red River.
ALB. H. LATTIMER, MARTIN PARMER, E. O. LEGRAND, STEPH. W. BLOUNT,	}	San Augustine.

SYD. O. PENNINGTON, W. CAR'L CRAWFORD,	}	Shelby.
JAMES POWER, SAM. HOUSTON, DAVID THOMAS, EDWARD CONRAD, JOHN TURNER,	}	Refugio.
		San Patricio.
B. BRIGGS GOODRICH, G. W. BARNETT, JAMES G. SWISHER, JESSE GRIMES,	}	Washington.

Printed by Baker and Bordens, San Felipe de Austin.

THE BATTLE OF SAN JACINTO

Volunteers continued to arrive from the United States to join the Texas army. By April 1836, Sam Houston's men numbered about 1,200. However, about 200 were too sick to fight. Santa Anna's army of 1,200 men forced them as far east as Galveston Bay.

On April 21, 1836, Houston decided to mount a surprise attack near the San Jacinto River. The Mexicans were trapped. The Texans overpowered them in under half an hour. About 600 Mexicans were killed. Hundreds more were captured, including Santa Anna. Amazingly, only nine of Houston's men died. About thirty were hurt. The Texas Revolution was over.

TIMELINE OF THE TEXAS REVOLUTION

October 2, 1835
Battle of Gonzales

October 28, 1835
Battle of Concepción

December 8, 1835
Texans take control of San Antonio

October 10, 1835
Battle of Goliad

November 26, 1835
Grass Fight

TEXAS

Colorado River

Brazos River

San Jacinto River

Washington-on-
the-Brazos ○

San Antonio   ○ Gonzales

★ San Jacinto

Grass Fight ★○★ *Alamo*

Galveston
Bay

Concepción

○ Goliad ★

Rio Grande

**GULF OF
MEXICO**

Key

- ○ city
- ★ battle

March 2, 1836	March 17, 1836
Texas Declaration of Independence	**Texas convention approves constitution**

February 23, 1836	March 6, 1836	April 21, 1836
Siege of Alamo begins	**Battle of the Alamo**	**Battle of San Jacinto**

23

THE REPUBLIC OF TEXAS

After the Battle of San Jacinto, Santa Anna signed two **treaties** with Texas. One promised that the Mexican army would move back across the Rio Grande. The second treaty set up trade between Texas and Mexico. It named the Rio Grande as the Texas-Mexico border. Both governments broke the treaties, but the fighting stopped.

Sam Houston was elected president of the **Republic** of Texas in 1836. The new nation was very poor. Other nations would not lend it money. It also needed a way to guard itself from Mexican and Native American raids. Houston believed that many problems could be solved through one event. The United States needed to annex Texas. However, in 1836, the United States refused. It feared a war with Mexico.

Sam Houston

The two treaties signed by Santa Anna were called the Treaties of Velasco. One treaty was kept secret for a time. It promised to let Santa Anna go free if he helped the Texans.

secret treaty

public treaty

Under the Texas constitution, a president couldn't serve two terms in a row. In 1838, Mirabeau B. Lamar became the second Texas president. Lamar worked to build a school system. Unlike Sam Houston, he wanted to move Native Americans out of Texas. He also worked to make the area now known as New Mexico a part of Texas.

Sam Houston easily won reelection in 1841. He tried to make peace treaties between settlers and Native Americans. He also avoided another war with Mexico in 1842. Houston continued to work toward the annexation of Texas by the United States.

The last president of the Republic of Texas was Anson Jones. He was elected in 1844. By this time, the United States wanted to annex Texas. Texas became part of the United States on December 29, 1845.

Mirabeau B. Lamar

This cartoon shows some American officials trying to stop Texas annexation. However, they were unsuccessful.

THE MEXICAN-AMERICAN WAR

After the United States annexed Texas, Mexico and the United States argued about the Texas border. Mexico claimed it was the Nueces River. The United States claimed it was the Rio Grande. The United States also wanted the Mexican territory that is today New Mexico and California. The Mexican government refused to talk to U.S. officials.

In May 1846, the Mexican-American War began. U.S. forces easily overpowered Mexican forces in California, New Mexico, and even Mexico. In February 1848, the Treaty of Guadalupe Hidalgo gave the United States more than 500,000 square miles (1,300,000 sq km) of Mexican land. It also made the Rio Grande the border between Texas and Mexico.

CAUSES AND EFFECTS OF THE TEXAS REVOLUTION

CAUSE
Texans wanted to be independent state

CAUSE
Texans wanted slavery

CAUSE
Texans didn't want to pay higher taxes

CAUSE
Santa Anna became dictator

EFFECT 1
Texas Revolution

EFFECT 2
Texas became republic

EFFECT 3
Texas became U.S. state

Through the Treaty of Guadalupe Hildago, Mexico gave up what are now the states of Utah, Nevada, California, and parts of Colorado, New Mexico, Arizona, Wyoming, and Texas.

READER RESPONSE PROJECTS

- The "come and take it" flag became an important part of the Texas Revolution. Choose another event in the Texas Revolution. Think of a flag that Texans could have used to stand for that event. Create your flag with poster board or cloth. Display it in the classroom.

- William Barret Travis wrote letters asking for troops to fight at the Alamo. His letters tell us about events within the Alamo. They also tell his feelings about the revolution. Imagine you are Travis. Write a letter to your family. Tell what you see, hear, and feel.

- Use this book, the Internet, or books at the library to find reasons for and against the Texas Revolution. Create a table that shows your findings. Then organize a talk between two groups of friends. Ask one group to talk for the Texas Revolution and the other group to talk against it.

GLOSSARY

constitution (kahn-stuh-TOO-shun) The basic rules by which a country or state is governed.

convention (kuhn-VEHN-shun) A formal meeting for some special purpose.

declaration (deh-kluh-RAY-shun) An official announcement.

dictator (DIHK-tay-tuhr) A person who takes power and has total control over others.

explorer (ihk-SPLOHR-uhr) Someone who travels to find new lands.

militia (muh-LIH-shuh) A group of ordinary people who are not soldiers but are trained and ready to fight when needed.

mission (MIH-shun) A place where church leaders teach their beliefs and help the community.

rebellion (rih-BEHL-yuhn) A fight against one's government.

religion (rih-LIH-juhn) A belief in a god or gods.

republic (rih-PUH-blihk) A form of government in which the authority belongs to the people.

revolution (reh-vuh-LOO-shun) A complete change in government brought about by force.

siege (SEEJ) Blocking off a fort or city with soldiers so that nothing can get in or go out.

surrender (suh-REHN-duhr) To give up.

treaty (TREE-tee) An official agreement, signed by each party.

INDEX

Due to the changing nature of Internet links, the Rosen Publishing Group, Inc., has developed an online list of Web sites related to the subject of this book. This site is updated regularly. Please use this link to access the list: **http://www.rcbmlinks.com/sot/texrev/**